Is It So If You Think It's So?

THOUGHTS ON TEACHING & PLAYING CHAMBER MUSIC

AN ANTI-MANUAL

Robert Merfeld

Cover Design: Peter Mendelsund

Is It So If You Think It's So?/Robert Merfeld - 1st ed.

ISBN-13: 978-0692901632

Contents

DEDICATION

To Anya

In 1989, I was fortunate enough to hear Mieczyslaw Horszowski play a wonderful piano recital at the tender age of 97 at the Longy School of Music in Cambridge, Massachusetts. Perhaps the inspiration for his luminous playing and rejuvenated career stemmed from his decision to get married for the first time in his life when he was 90. Years later I met his lovely wife, the Italian pianist Bice Horszowski and had the pleasure of reading the Schubert F Minor Fantasy with her.

Two years ago, I too, got married for the first time in my life, to Anya Shemetyeva, who is the inspiration for what I have written in these pages and the spirit that lies behind them. As one of my closest friends said at our wedding, "It was certainly worth the wait."

ACKNOWLEDGEMENTS

To **Leonid Hambro**, *my childhood piano teacher, who, while honoring what was on the page, relished the act of bringing it to life and instilled in me the joy of listening.*

To **Emil Danenberg**, *my teacher at Oberlin, who was equally fanatical about music and sports, having studied with Arnold Schönberg at UCLA while Jackie Robinson was the star tailback on the football team. He taught me the joy of discipline and craftsmanship - to protect my talent.*

To **Stanley Ritchie**, *who took my childhood love for Bach, Mozart and Schubert and opened up new ways to explore this music - helping me realize that inquiry need not separate from the heart.*

To **Bayla Keyes**, *with whom I have played well over fifty duo-sonatas (including all the violin sonatas of Bach, Bartók, Brahms and Mozart), who symbolizes much of what I have written in these pages - trust, openness and music-making coming from a source of true friendship.*

To **Ellen Lowery**, *with thanks and gratitude, who occasionally reminds me of how many years we have shared a friendship, starting with piano lessons at Windham College in Putney, Vermont way back in 1974. She remembers concerts I can't even recall playing and now has spent innumerable hours helping me transfer the chaos of my scribbled notes onto her computer, as well as scanning the musical examples found here. Without her encouragement, it is unlikely this project would have come to fruition.*

INTRODUCTION

I HAVE THOUGHT MANY times that there is a book to be written about the teaching of chamber music and the sociology of chamber music interactions. On occasion, I have been encouraged by students to consider this project, but have been reluctant, mainly because the prospect of taking the fluid and improvisatory aspects of teaching and fixing them into an unchangeable context has felt unappealing. When asked, "Who are you writing for?" I remain to an extent uncertain. I set out merely to write, not for an intended audience, not to necessarily fashion a book.

Often, as artists, our work is directed towards an upcoming concert or show. To work simply for the pleasure of the work itself has become too rare an experience. As the process of this "anti-manual" evolved, I became increasingly convinced that I needed to share my ideals with those who care about how we listen to each other in this often discouraging world and those who view education as a breeding ground for creativity and curiosity rather than cloning and dogma. Although, over the years, I have enjoyed feedback from painters as much as fellow musicians, I do recognize that the non-musician may not respond to all of the musical examples cited in the upcoming pages as might a practicing musician. I am not a scientist, but do remember when reading *Moby Dick* years ago, that every word of the elaborate scientific explanations became inescapably part of the overall experience.

Books such as Arnold Steinhardt's *Violin Dreams* and Anner Bylsma's *Bach, the Fencing Master* received well-deserved attention, partly due to the distinguished careers of the authors. Is the fact that my life has followed quite a different trajectory even relevant to the nature of this endeavor? Now that I have virtually stopped performing, I have a heightened passion for teaching and the sharing of ideas, which has lent a sense of purpose to my choosing to write, to compose, to stay immersed in what I love. For me, designations such as "teacher" and "master class" have inherent issues, most of which emanate from "I impart - you receive" or even "I know - you don't". Perhaps a reason for writing this book is to dispel that notion and to set down the ideas I care so deeply about, some of which end up being recurrent even if modified or altered over time.

Perhaps this is also to express gratitude to all those who have shared their curiosity about and thirst for music with me for all these years at Harvard University, Boston University, the Longy School of Music of Bard College and a variety of summer programs, including Boston University's Tanglewood Institute,the Garth Newel Music Center and the Center for Chamber Music at Apple Hill, which I helped found in 1970, resigning 25 years later after a rich if tumultuous attempt at musical democracy.

Two wonderful musicians who read my manuscript with great care and gave me a wealth of feedback were Stanley Ritchie and Richard Goode. Their encouragement inspired me to get this book "out there" and share it with fellow music lovers. Over the years, if someone were to come up to me after a concert and say, "You sounded great", I would experience a mild sense of satisfaction, but if that person said, "You do love music", my heart would skip a beat. Richard expressed the hope that I would keep on writing, adding on to what I had started. He had some reservations about my original title, "*It Is So, If You Think It's So*", because it could be interpreted in a way which might be at odds with my "distrust of authority". He suggested "*It Ain't Necessarily So, Even If You Think It Is*" as a possibility. So, even though I view the original title as a reflection of how perception is endlessly subjective, and a rejection of the absolute, I decided that posing a question in the title (Is It So...?) came closest to the underlying intention of the book.

CHAPTER ONE

"Not Knowing"

YEARS AGO, I SAW a quote by the dance choreographer Agnes DeMille, the gist of which was that creativity and great art come from "not knowing, from taking leap after leap in the dark, not knowing where one might land but leaping nonetheless". Perhaps "not knowing" allows us to be open and to be surprised where paths might lead us. It might mean that, even after fifty years of playing and teaching countless works of music, at any moment the idea that I am inviting others (be they students, colleagues, or listeners) to consider may be embraced, rejected or put on hold. Certainly after a lifetime spent with music, I would imagine that there is an accumulated reservoir of experience which includes response to melody, rhythm, structure, harmony, boundaries of style, etc. But how fascinating it is that as experience grows, certainty may be viewed with suspicion.

When playing music with others, conviction can lead us astray if "knowing" makes us blind to what someone else might imagine. In summoning up the courage to walk out on stage, we try to convince ourselves that we "know" what we are about to play, but presenting what we love and have labored over is not truly an end-point, but rather part of an ongoing process. Recently, a violist and pianist were playing for me the first movement of the Brahms F Minor Sonata and where there is a modulation into E major they took a generous amount of time. When I asked them about it, the pianist said they had decided to place the second beat (marked *dolce*) late.

First movement E major modulation, Brahms F Minor Viola (or Clarinet) Sonata, Op. 120 no. 1

I urged them not to predetermine the poetics of music and had them actually try putting the second beat early. This was not about establishing a preference but rather retaining an openness of approach. They tried this alternative quite convincingly although the pianist did so begrudgingly - unfortunately, the world of ego often seems to intrude. The leader who "knows" tends to prefer decision-making and to say, "You are late" or "You are behind me" instead of "We're not together".

Last Christmas Eve, I was chatting with the pastor at a Lutheran Church where I was to perform in an hour's time and expressed my admiration for two sermons I heard him deliver the previous Easter, full of certainty about the Resurrection but remarkably different in their inflection, choice of language and imagery. He said to me, "After forty years it is a way of staying fresh, and I love what I do." If this pastor is an improviser, what is it we do when playing or coaching Schubert's "Trout" Quintet for the umpteenth time? When asked what he thought about adding embellishments to the repeats of dance movements in Bach Suites, the Dutch cellist Anner Bylsma said, in a conversation with Tim Janoff, "Maybe when I know a bit more - for now, I prefer to change the pronunciation" (both more modest than what one might expect, and more interesting as well). Perhaps what he is recognizing is the impossibility of improving on Bach.

All sorts of intriguing questions arise here. What is it we improvise as classical musicians, and if aesthetics are in flux, how can teaching dare to impose single solutions? Recently, I have wracked my brain trying to find any absolute musical phrase or gesture which can only be played one way, and so far it seems non-existent. Put on multiple recordings of the first four notes of Beethoven's Fifth Symphony or of the first two measures of Schubert's *Death & the Maiden* Quartet and notice the dissimilarities. They are there.

Some years ago, while waiting for my car to be serviced at a dealership, I met a psychiatrist from South Africa and we got to talking about what we did in our lives. Finding out that I was a musician, he said, "I guess what I do, also, is to listen - when people truly listen it is an act of love or friendship." There exists a kind of mythology that athletes or musicians, who might have an antipathy towards each other still may bond to accomplish remarkable results. Yet, if one has a question, as a member of a string quartet or a sports team, whether playing with friends makes for a more rewarding experience, I imagine the answer is obvious - good chemistry does matter. Since there is an intimacy - almost beyond marriage - which is inevitable when on tour day after day, constantly interacting, a certain amount of space "offstage" can be essential. I think this need for privacy can give a false impression of alienation. Tension or conflict, if harnessed positively, can, however, breed creativity. Disagreement within a group, especially when exploring a composer like Beethoven, can be a vital component of a fertile working process. If there is a link between listening and friendship, then playing music with friends can be both extraordinary and immediate, in the sense that people who have just met can feel as though they have known each other forever by simply reading a Mozart sonata together. Because of friendship, one can experience the pleasure of enjoying playing something very differently than previously imagined because your partner encouraged you in that direction. There are moments in chamber music when the antennae of awareness are so present that it becomes inconceivable that things won't be together, that sounds won't mesh sympathetically. This thought of people breathing together, their sounds blending, somehow feels inescapably linked to friendship and kindness. I, as a pianist at such a moment, am not merely trying to find a way to blend with the sound of a violin, but also to join with the spirit of its player. Empathy can be so powerful that a pianist can help violinists play in tune simply by making them comfortable or can feel as though an out of tune note is something that he missed himself. Behind all this is something sociological in a very elemental way.

After many, many years of playing both chamber music and pick-up games of soccer and hockey, I find the cross-connections uncanny. What is fluid, graceful, shared, or undecided is common to both arenas. Unfortunately, the hierarchies and judgments that separate people are there also. The violinist who needs to predominate, who knows how a passage of music must go, regardless of the needs of his colleagues, is so similar to the basketball or soccer player who will only pass as a last resort and then only to the one deemed most worthy instead of the less experienced player who is wide open. Why be a soloist when you are part of a quartet or, say, in basketball, a quintet? Is it the need to predominate?

CHAPTER TWO

Shared Perception & Responsibility

It is fascinating how territorial and narrow musicians' perceptions can be. In my teaching, if I ask violinists if pianists talk to them about intonation or bow speed, or ask singers whether pianists explore the poetry with them, or if I ask pianists if singers or string players talk to them about pedaling, the answer tends to be "almost never". The point is, for me, that in chamber music ultimately all choices become shared choices and shared responsibility.

I remember, years ago, hearing a world-famous quartet play Schubert's *Death & the Maiden* and the first violinist seemed to be making unforgivably glib choices over and over. I sat there thinking that his colleagues needed to tell him, "You can't do that", or "That slide sounds artificial". There is a problem here, however. The so-called perpetrator may, in fact, be communicating from a place that is totally sincere, but because we think the choice made violates our sense of the music, we assume it is not genuine.

Shared responsibility in chamber music could also be viewed as shared perception. Much of this has to do with the internalization of other players' processes rather than externalization. What this means is that the non-string player actually feels the sensation of a bow change, a shift or a slide, the non-wind player feels the difference in how sound speaks or how it tapers, be it on a flute, oboe or horn. As a pianist or conductor it can drive you crazy trying to reconcile the desire for a chord to have a soft palette, cushioned entry with a horn player's need to have a more specific "attack". The difference in timbres between instruments is both fascinating and obvious. In playing or coaching works for piano and winds, such as the Mozart or Beethoven Quintets or the Poulenc Sextet, it is quickly apparent that a pianist needs totally different sound approaches depending on which instrument is being related to. Generally, the horn might ask for more support and more sound than is suggested by the intimacy of the bassoon - the flute, especially in lower registers, might ask for something gentler and more dispersed, and the clarinet might have the widest range of possibilities from a whisper to a howl. One of the reasons the Brahms Clarinet Quintet is so extraordinary is that the clarinet can lie in the middle of a dark B minor chord (for instance at the very end of the quintet), almost becoming an honorary second viola, or it can wail out its improvisation in the slow movement in a manner which could make John Coltrane seem tame.

In Alfred Brendel's wonderful book *Thoughts & Afterthoughts,* he writes at length about how pianists may imitate the sound and attacks of other instruments. And this includes the singer's world of vowels and consonants. It can be very rewarding for a violinist to think of the E string in relation to an E vowel, or lower strings in relation to darker vowels. Likewise, imagine a bow change or the beginning of any chord which attempts to coordinate with the word "king" - a hard consonant as opposed to the word "sleep" which is softer and takes longer to say (even more so in German: *schlummer*). Language becomes more all-inclusive and less specific to one's own idiomatic territory.

With this in mind, I find it more interesting, when coaching a piece such as the Brahms Horn Trio, to encourage the players to explore what links their approach rather than what differentiates it. Ultimately, we all breathe and breathing is not merely a way to get sufficient oxygen, it communicates how we hear the music. If breathing has character and quality, then certainly so does our sense of pulse and how we count. Try and get two people - they don't have to be musicians - to count out loud to four, one counting crisply, one languidly - it is very hard to be together. If music has mood and flexibility, so does its underlying pulse, which is one reason I distrust and even detest metronomes, another being that they can become a substitute for actually listening. A while ago, I asked a class working on Brahms duo-sonatas, "If you were to take a random sampling of one hundred passages from Bach to Brahms, how many might conform to "strict tempo"? One violinist, with a rather whimsical spirit, said softly, "perhaps ten". A pianist with a much more doctrinaire outlook, said, categorically, "at least fifty". I knew what my choice might have been, but left it unspoken. The inherent danger here, for one disinclined to provide answers, lies in asking questions hoping for a particular response. Is there a contradiction here? "Not knowing", having a willingness to perhaps be wrong, must include both teacher and student.

CHAPTER THREE

𝄐

"It Is So If You Think It's So"

Some of the thoughts which have arisen so far link kindness to awareness and openness to multiple possibilities at any moment. In college, I took a fantastic modern drama course and remember reading a Luigi Pirandello play with the title *It Is So, If You Think It's So.* Could this not be the perfect motto for all variables in interpretative outlook or for the way musicians can be magicians as we weave our webs of illusion? Think about the possibility that all music is about perpetual motion, with the exception of dramatic silences where you actually choose to stop. Perpetual motion can be how we fill space musically and physically, and legato can become more about how we listen than what we do. Take the title of this play and apply it to rehearsal behavior - let's say someone thinks you are rushing or are a bit out of tune - you don't agree, but step back and say to yourself, "There must be a reason for their reaction". Apply it to a pianist making a crescendo on a chord already struck, convincing us that it is actually happening through body movement. Apply it to the second of Schumann's Fantasy Pieces, Op. 73 where the opening melody wants to be presented similarly as it passes from the keyboard right hand to the clarinet (or cello) entry. The trick, for a pianist, is to make the melodic rhythm sound like a quarter note followed by two eighth notes, seemingly a mathematical impossibility since the second eighth note is also functioning as the third note of the triplet. It is possible to create the illusion that both rhythms maintain their identity by playing the second note of the triplet in a veiled and slightly ambiguous manner.

Opening of the second movement, Schumann Fantasy Pieces, Op. 73 for clarinet (or cello) and piano

Apply this to my experience with a touching Korean pianist several years ago playing the first movement of the Bach

G Major Sonata for Violin & Keyboard. After she had finished a wonderful reading of it with her partner, I noticed a harpsichord in the corner of the room and asked her if she might enjoy trying it. She said that she had never touched a harpsichord but would be delighted. This second reading was even more amazing, especially considering it was a one-manual instrument. Not only was she open to the experience, but she was able to create the illusion of a quieter "B" section. With the same registration she did sound softer and more intimate than she had in the festive opening section. How could she do this? Ask Pirandello! A while later, I ran across her at a pizza shop and joined her and some of her friends for lunch. After a bit, I said to her, "You know, this is probably the first time we've ever really had a conversation, but I feel that somehow I know you because your playing is so generous." I'll never forget her answer: *"That's what I love about music."*

CHAPTER FOUR

Modesty

Is THE ROLE OF a teacher to provide answers or to ask questions, to present possibilities or even perhaps learn from the exchange of ideas? Recently I heard a wonderful interview with Ian McKellen, the distinguished elderly British actor, who was describing what a joy it was to be on stage or in films with actors in their twenties and to realize that they knew everything he did and that he could learn from them. Humility, I would say, not humiliation. To witness modesty in those who have attained prominence is sadly an uncommon experience. Perhaps the seeking of preeminence creates hierarchal attitudes which threaten artistic purity.

Some years ago, I was teaching at a summer festival at which a renowned string player was a guest. A student cellist was playing a Brandenburg Concerto with him and expressed to me her gratitude for how collegial he was. I agreed, but remember saying to her, "Why shouldn't he be?" A day or two later, that same girl performed Beethoven's Op. 59 no. 3 string quartet and perhaps the fugue did, at times, lose control. After the concert, I was chatting with this distinguished musician (whose company and collaboration I too had truly enjoyed) and he said to me, "They haven't learned how to breathe yet". I didn't particularly agree, but that is not what disturbed me. What seemed implicit in his comment was: "They haven't learned how to breathe yet, but I have, and some day with some luck and hard work............." To this day I wonder if I mistakenly read condescension into his remark. Why would I have preferred: "Damn, that fugue was rushed"? Any of us could say that often enough about ourselves. Another memorable interview I recall was with the German mezzo-soprano Christa Ludwig, years ago, in which she described what it is in music we aspire to and maybe find once or twice a year. This world famous singer said the lesson for her was to be grateful for those rare, transcendent moments and, while continuing to strive, not to berate yourself when falling short.

In chamber music, perhaps the opposite of this modesty is what you find in Schönberg's *Verklaerte Nacht* or Tchaikovsky's *Souvenirs de Florence.* To talk here about overstatement, self-indulgence or bloatedness may offend some lovers of these pieces, but I am willing. What happened to music, especially in Germany at the end of the nineteenth century, makes me appreciate even more the modesty of Dvorák, and yearn for what is pristine in late Fauré. The simple G major scale, played by the strings in the slow movement of the Fauré Second Piano Quintet is more touching to me than the admittedly beautiful, ethereal conclusion to the Schönberg because its modesty is symbolic of the whole.

From the third movement, Fauré Piano Quintet in C Minor, Op. 115

CHAPTER FIVE

The Objective - Subjective Quandary

If music, in all its nuances and stylistic challenges, cannot be reduced to single correct solutions, then what we offer should recognize this as we attempt to provide guidance. One could argue that there are objective - subjective boundaries that affect the whole conversation. The problem here is that the determination of what is objective or subjective is, to begin with, subjective. Consider the issues of intonation or balance in chamber music. When is a note or a chord out of tune beyond a doubt? Is it when nine out of ten discerning listeners would agree that it is so? When is there a balance problem in a Beethoven piano & violin sonata? There are times when a pianist clearly "drowns out" his partner and virtually all listeners would recognize this. There are times when a string player overshoots a shift and an undeniable mistake has occurred. In neither case is the most creative conversation likely to ensue. Where intonation or balance becomes fascinating is when different choices might affect the aesthetic picture, but not necessarily to correct something gone wrong. I remember discussing intonation with Marc Johnson of the Vermeer Quartet out at Tanglewood and mentioning that I hear thirds lower in A-flat major than in A major because of the luxuriousness of the key. I am not sure he agreed, but these are the kinds of questions that make intonation so intriguing - like the places where string players don't necessarily need to conform to the immovable nature of piano pitch.

If one expects the role of the piano in a Brahms cello sonata to be subordinate or deferential, then simply seeing the piano open with full stick would have many listeners predisposed to something problematic. This is even truer playing for singers where text is paramount. In the case where the piano is overwhelming, could the problem be because of acoustics, or non-matching kinds of sound, or merely one person imposing his will in a deal-with-it kind of way? Balance issues can be so intriguing in a movement like the finale of the Brahms E Minor Cello Sonata where there is the rationality of seeking contrapuntal clarity and the less rational aspect of struggle and testing of the boundaries of what a cello can cope with (including registration limitations).

From the Finale, Brahms E Minor Cello Sonata, Op. 38

Where is a given figure an accompanying, non-intrusive texture behind the melody (perhaps the opening of Beethoven's "Spring" Sonata) - where is it non-accommodating and rather the rhythmic motivation for the music's energy (the Finale of Beethoven's A Major Cello Sonata)? Often the lack of a clear answer contains the essence of the exploratory process.

Allegro, Beethoven "Spring" Sonata, Op. 24

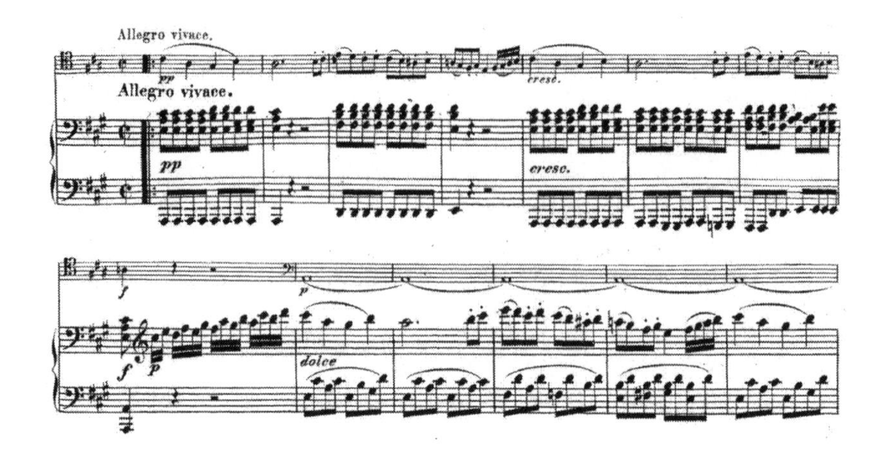

Finale, Beethoven A Major Cello Sonata, Op. 69

There are multiple reasons, in rehearsal or teaching, I prefer to say to someone, “I'd like that G-sharp a bit higher” or “This passage is losing rhythmic stability”, rather than “You are flat” or “You are rushing”. To begin with, the latter makes the person being addressed feel accused, which never helps, and assumes that the one offering the reaction is right, which is not necessarily the case.

CHAPTER SIX

𝄐

Music & Math

One could say that to solve a rhythmically intricate passage in a Bartók string quartet requires a particular logical solution. This reminds me of the time I was about to coach chamber music in the basement of Harvard University's Music Department and a Pakistani security guard - sitting at his desk studying the Koran - asked me if I thought music was about mathematics. "At times", I remember answering. Speaking of math, counting measures to figure out the shapes of phrases, to discover what is symmetrical and what is not, to notice where phrases are extended, overlapped or shortened, is a process critical to understanding logic in music, especially Beethoven. Counting measures helps us find pulse in music as well as natural and unnatural stress. In the trio section of the Scherzo from Beethoven's "Harp" Quartet, it reveals that the true "downbeat" of the four measure units is the second played measure, not the first. It reveals that the cello's first measure is actually a pick-up to the following metric units and makes the viola's entrance likewise start on a preparatory beat, making the harmonic suspensions afterwards land on strong beats.

Trio section from the Scherzo of Beethoven "Harp" String Quartet, Op. 74

In the waltz from Dvorák's String Serenade, it probably has us counting in five, not what one would expect. Even if you consider the first measure as a pickup to the next four measures, the recurrent bass pattern clearly is a five measure unit starting from the E on the first downbeat.

Waltz, Dvorák String Serenade in E Major, Op. 22

In the last movement of Fauré's G Minor Piano Quartet, Op. 45 (a wonderful work not heard often enough), counting measures might help us realize that the almost processional viola/cello passage has its own meter in three measure units while the more secular, fluid violin solo has its own duple meter.

From the last movement, Fauré G Minor Piano Quartet, Op. 45

The connection between math and music reminds me, too, of my childhood piano teacher, Leonid Hambro, and his fascination with the Fibonacci numbers and how they might relate to proportions in Bartók. His brilliance had him playing chess against Bobby Fisher on TV, learning the Hindemith Piano Concerto overnight and even getting kicked out of Las Vegas for figuring out how to beat the card dealers. There are moments of logic in music-making where an ensemble tracks a crescendo or accelerando totally in sync, or likewise matches the properties of sound (density, hollowness, etc.). These moments of supreme logic often can grant us a surprising degree of emotional satisfaction, which makes it increasingly difficult to separate them from the aesthetic experience.

CHAPTER SEVEN

"That's Better" "You Need To"

CONSIDER THE SIMPLE ACT of how a pianist invites the violin entry at the beginning of the first Brahms Violin Sonata with two G major chords. Are they anti-gravity, are they voiced upward, is the gesture in one, are they more reverent or awakened, are they "*vivace*" of a sort? What a wonderful responsibility to invite, to influence, but hopefully without controlling what comes next.

Brahms Sonata for Piano & Violin in G Major, Op. 78

If music is so full of variable choices, then the two catchphrases in master classes that feel misguided and condescending are, "That's better" and "You need to....". Several years ago, a wonderful Japanese student brought the B Major Prelude & Fugue from the first book of Bach's *Well-Tempered Clavier* to a lesson with me. I was totally taken with her reading of it, which essentially had a leisurely prelude and a more lively fugue. After expressing appreciation - which we often forget to do - I had her invert the tempo relationships and both of us found the result equally satisfying - which shows that answering the frequently asked question, "How fast or how slow should this go" is elusive or hopefully so.

Let's look at a handful of examples that may help elucidate the musical conversation. I remember working with a group on the Shostakovich Seventh Quartet, written in memory of his wife, who had just died. We were experimenting with the opening fragments being disembodied, cut adrift, and lost in space, allowing the Scherzo later on to transform the motifs into something totally the opposite.

Opening of Shostakovich Quartet no. 7

From the third movement, Shostakovich Quartet no. 7

Playing in a master class the group was informed that their approach to the opening needed to be more incisive, even malignant, and then, having done so satisfactorily were told, "That's better". If we have any modesty as teachers, I beg us to present options and then ask, "What do you think?" For that group playing Shostakovich, the result was not better, but closer to what the person leading the class wanted, and undoubtedly different. Another time a group working on Schubert's *Quartettsatz* was playing the opening in a non-visceral, searching manner, more melancholy than stormy (perhaps akin to the opening of the "Unfinished" Symphony) and was told, in a class, that it "needed to be much faster and restlessly agitated". The group never truly recovered from the imposition of what was deemed "right".

Opening, Schubert Quartettsatz, D. 703

Countless times, I have heard students play something that I will ask a question about and their response is, "My teacher told me to play it that way", or "That's the way they did it on the recording" - or a violist, after an especially sexy slide in Schubert's "Arpeggione" Sonata saying, "My teacher told me to ham it up". I would encourage students to imagine themselves in a very gentle musical court of law where they have to defend all their intentions. After a group I had worked with performed the Dvorák Viola Quintet, the first violinist mentioned to me that his teacher, who was at the concert, thought he rushed into the first variation of the variation movement. Maybe it was so, but it seemed to symbolize the objective/ subjective quandary. If the 32nd notes in the first violin part are activated and a bit unsettled, the variation might start earlier than if the music is viewed more wistfully - which is right? If the players convey their ideas with conviction, the listener can be swayed by a variety of realizations.

From the variation movement, Dvorák Viola Quintet, Op.97

One of the inherent challenges in teaching is, if the piece we are coaching is a work we likely have both played and taught countless times, how do we retain a freshness of approach, a jazz musician's inclination towards improvisation? We need to remain, as Bylsma describes himself, archaeologists of music, searching for what we imagine composers had in mind while realizing more often than not there are multiple possibilities as we explore the language of music. Even though listening to Bartók play his own music is astonishing and revealing, to try to play it the same way would totally miss the point of what makes it so wonderful.

Let's look at the openings of two chamber works, the Mozart G Minor Viola Quintet and Schubert's A Minor String Quartet, which are among my favorites:

Opening, Mozart G Minor Viola Quintet, K. 516

Opening, Schubert A Minor String Quartet, D. 804

It so happens that I hear both of them as being infinitely sad in a non-turbulent, non-restless way. In this resigned state, time travels more slowly, the spaces between melodic fragments widen and the articulations soften. The second violin strands in the Schubert become timeless and the drum beats in the viola and cello become more like sighs, consuming whole bows. Maybe, despite myself, I would plead, when teaching, for this gentleness to prevail, and can hear myself making the attempt. However, I am convinced that creative teaching would notice and encourage a group that sensed more anxiety, helping them make choices which communicate that - activating the accompanying patterns, making the breath marks melodically less spacious, moving the tempi forward, etc. Perhaps there can be a similar pleasure here as when enjoying a performance where the interpretation is dramatically at odds with your conception of the piece.

If one does not assume agreement with the ideas one offers as a teacher, the creative process can become heightened albeit wonderfully inefficient. At Harvard, years ago, I was working with a group on the late Schubert G Major String Quartet, and some of the same players had worked with me earlier on the Schubert Cello Quintet.

Opening, Schubert G Major String Quartet, D. 887

Opening, Schubert C Major Cello Quintet, D. 956

As I remember it, most of us agreed that the opening of the quintet is essentially vocal, the *crescendo* blossoming, expectant but not disturbing. However, the arguments over the quartet's opening raged on for weeks before we all realized that we would never make it through the whole piece unless we pushed on. My thought was that the first G major triad has immediate tension before it explodes into minor - the least sensitive major-minor relationship ever to be found in Schubert - an anti-vocal statement followed by a series of jagged Beethovenian fragments. Well, the first violinist in particular thought the first chord should start with the same outlook as the C major chord at the beginning of the quintet, which would make what comes afterwards more startling. There was also the feeling that jaggedness and angularity do not fit Schubert, which is exactly, for me, what makes the piece extraordinary. Now, years later, it is easier for me to remember the fertility of the working process than how they actually ended up playing the places in question.

As I mentioned in the introduction, one of the inherent problems with committing one's ideas to pen and paper is that the ideas become fixed and the element of surprise may suffer as a result. If I hear myself, when teaching, repeating something I recall saying in the past I am usually disappointed. Even if a chosen adjective is particularly apt, let's say describing the piano and viola texture early on in the Shostakovich Piano Quintet as bleak, I can feel my imagination wilt if unable to experience it freshly.

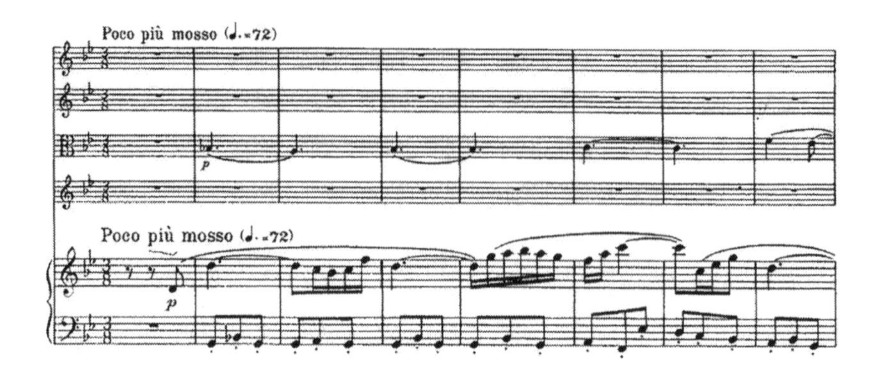

From the Shostakovich G Minor Piano Quintet, Op. 57

Although the physics of playing an instrument may lend itself more to a systematic approach, the poetics of music seem invariably more fluid. The problem here is that the boundary between physics and aesthetics is also fluid. I would start by saying that our choices of fingerings and bowings are both aesthetic and physical choices - they can seek comfort and, at times, even seek discomfort and they relate to the unique physiology of any given player, the size of their hands, the shape of their fingers, etc. Again, it is a conversation we can return to, but for now, I would say that if it is inconceivable for any two people to play a work of Bach the same way, it is equally inconceivable that any two people would choose the same fingerings (unless told to by their teachers). What makes it all the more frustrating is that supposedly scholarly editions like Henle feel a need to include fingerings, especially in Bach's keyboard writing where there are no indicated tempos or articulations - yet articulations and tempos are at the heart of fingering choices.

Before expanding on the joy of surprise in teaching, I find myself wondering if the fact that certain concepts crop up over and over lends validity to them and thereby adds purpose to my writing. Perhaps this will be discovered as I proceed. In any case, unlike Brahms, I have not thrown anything in the wastebasket just yet. There is a pleasure in rambling, in daydreaming, which reminds me of many wonderful illogical passages in Dvorák chamber music where, all of a sudden, something materializes which does not quite fit, but you have the feeling he is on a walk, has an idea and decides to use it for fear of losing it.

CHAPTER EIGHT

Surprise & Experimentation

One day, years ago, the director of the music department at one of the schools where I was teaching at the time saw me in the hallway and said, "I hear your course needs more structure" - not a word about what was actually being offered. I am not sure bureaucrats appreciate the idea of a teacher offering an experiment, not knowing what might transpire but then being delighted if - without expectations - a difference has been made.

Here, as I try to recall some of these attempts that proved gratifying, are a handful of examples, realizing of course that along the way there were failures as well. In no way would I suggest that these are experiments that others should try, much as I would urge musicians not to "decide" upon their freedoms, lest the freedom vanish.

- Working with an amateur clarinetist at a workshop on the Bartók *Contrasts*, I found that he was doing wonderfully until the challenging solo cadenza at the end of the first movement, which seemed beyond him. I had him try improvising a cadenza roughly acknowledging Bartók's patterns and style. He came up with something remarkably free and afterwards was actually able to navigate Bartók's cadenza with renewed confidence.
- Working with a group on the first Brahms Viola Quintet, we came upon a place at the end of the second movement where a spinning ornamental passage transfers from first viola alone to first viola and second violin and then to both violins. In the remote key of C-sharp minor, the playing was hopelessly out of tune and the flexibility needed to match the freedom within the seven note pattern was not happening. I had them try the same set of relationships, still seeking flexibility, but simply playing, instead, ascending and descending C major scales, and subsequently the passage began to work. A possible motto here - find a simplified model from which to build confidence.

From the slow movement, Brahms F Major Viola Quintet, Op. 88

- A pianist was playing for me the first movement of the late Schubert A Major Sonata - everything clean and musical but somehow a little generic and lacking imagination. We picked two pages and I had her scan the music with her fingertip and stop every time she saw something out of the ordinary - a special harmony, a rhythmic quirk, a change of texture, etc. Then I had her play again and find a way to acknowledge or reveal the places that had caught her fancy. The change was pretty astonishing - the lesson here may be don't tell people where the interesting harmonies or features are or what to do with them - just encourage the search.

- One of the things that distinguishes chamber music from orchestra playing is that the members of a quartet or quintet sit so close to each other that spatial separation is harder to imagine. I hear the first violin part in the opening of the slow movement of the Schubert Cello Quintet as somehow not belonging to the ensemble. Its angelic quality seems less present and more ethereal. Perhaps this is why only the inner vocies are marked *espressivo*. One day, during a coaching, I had the first violinist go out into the hallway and play her part with the group staying in place. The transformation was magical and when returning to their normal seating, the memory of what had transpired allowed a retention of that spatial sensation.

Opening of the slow movement, Schubert Cello Quintet, D. 956

- A pianist was struggling with the opening of the Scherzo of the Brahms B Major Trio, sounding unclear and rhythmically flabby. I had him close the lid that covers the keys and drum the passage with his knuckles. Immediately he found perfect clarity, which then easily transferred to his next reading of the passage. A thought here - when seeking pure rhythm, drumming may be the closest thing to an answer.

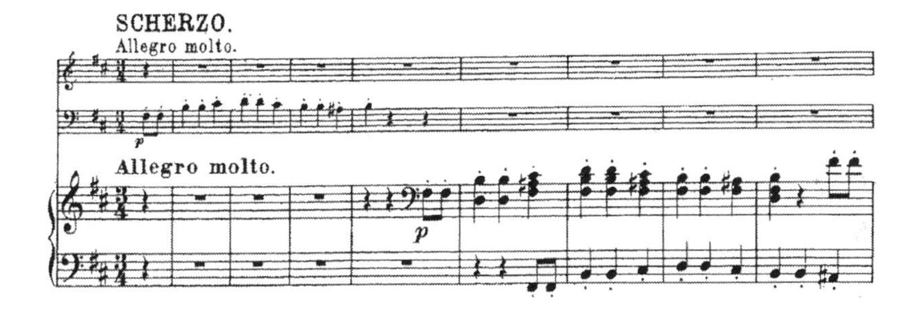

Opening of the Scherzo, Brahms B Major Piano Trio, Op. 8

Let's consider two more examples, which I hope are not too many. (Sometimes, when I teach, I'll say, for instance, in long transitional passages in Dvorák or Tchaikovsky, that we need a little red flag to warn us when boredom might set in, but if we stay engaged the listener has a good chance to keep us company):

- Here is an alternative to Bylsma's suggestion with respect to adding ornamentation in repeats (in this case the Adagio variation of the last movement of Mozart's "G Major/Minor" Violin Sonata, K. 379.

From the Adagio variation of the last movement,
Mozart "G Major/Minor" Violin Sonata, K. 379

If what a composer left us to play the first time through is already wildly florid and improvisatory, there is really nothing to add and to do it twice may seem contrived. One could, as Bylsma says, alter pronunciation, but in this case I suggested what could be attempted might be a reduction, a paring down of Mozart's fantastic detail the first time through and then play the florid version as the repeat - surely a difficult experiment to carry out on the spot, but intriguing for the right party. This is likely part of the equation - one has the tendency to offer experiments to those who have the curiosity to welcome experimentation.

- One such student did something I remember fondly in a class where I was asking how we respond to composers' choice of keys. This boy did a short (maybe 8-measure) improvisation in A major in more or less classical style. The presentation was basically quite sprightly. Then I asked him if he remembered what he had just played sufficiently to play it in A-flat major. He did, and what came out was more spacious, more luxurious, softer in articulation, and more pedaled. When I thanked him, he smiled and said, "How did you know A-flat major is my favorite key?"

A wonderful way, I have found, to discover one's associations with the properties of keys is to ask someone to move a passage from the original key to any other. Each key has its own personality and colorations that can affect tempo, warmth and types of attack. Playing something in the "wrong" key and then coming home to the intended key can be illuminating. This can be tricky and puzzling in the case of songs where so often singers and pianists are transposing to keys which are not original. For instance, virtually all of

Schubert's songs were written for high voice (tenor or soprano) and a whole generation of us fell in love with *Die Winterreise*, hearing Fischer-Dieskau live and in recording but not in Schubert's imagined keys. He sings the last "Organ-grinder" song of *Die Winterreise* in G minor, a rather dark key with a very different timbre than the two original keys which Schubert wavered between (B minor and A minor). Imagine the Schubert A Minor Quartet, whose opening we looked at before, in G minor and what a different piece it would become. I remember once, coaching a baritone and pianist on the last song of Schumann's *Dichterliebe* in which the severity and heartbreak of the opening C-sharp minor section yields to an achingly comforting piano postlude, or epilogue, in D-flat major. I knew they were in transposed keys, but because I was reading from a tenor edition, I did not realize that their edition unfortunately had this ending in B major, not C-flat major. Something felt wrong and it became clear why - what a difference between multiple flats and multiple sharps.

Music doesn't necessarily beg for description or adjectives, but I surely remember coaching the end of the Agitato movement of Schumann's A Major Op. 41 no. 3 quartet where there is a wonderful alternation back and forth between E-flat and F-sharp major, two very different keys, which the players did not seem to be acknowledging. When I asked them about it, the sixteen year-old first violinist reflected, then said,"F-sharp major.......I see the sky."

From the Agitato movement, Schumann A Major Quartet, Op. 41 no. 3

CHAPTER NINE

Songs as Chamber Music

I WOULD BE REMISS, in writing about memories and thoughts about chamber music, not to include a little section about the world of song. My most affectionate memory of my time spent at the Juilliard School was playing songs, especially Schubert and Schumann, in the studio of Hans Heinz, an old, beloved Viennese tenor who taught this literature as true chamber music, and did not allow singers to be in love with their own voices at the expense of caring for the poetry. I will never forget taking a walk with him and his wife (after many years of marriage, still calling her "my little angel") in the woods adjoining our hundred-acre farm in New Hampshire joined by our neighbor, a crusty, subsistence-level farmer who played a little violin and sax and was the exact same age as this distinguished voice teacher. I walked behind them a pace and listened to Howard McDonald describing every tree and every animal track to Hans Heinz and then to the patient explanation made to the farmer of how vibrato works - two people from totally opposite worlds equally in love with life and fascinated by each other. The last time I saw Heinz in his New York apartment I could not be sure if he recognized me, but I have lingering memories of him standing by the piano gesticulating, pleading for an inflection in a song and of him at the dinner table, his eyes gleaming with pleasure as we ate his wife's special Viennese pastries he was no longer allowed to enjoy. Aside from our common love for lieder, especially Schubert, perhaps we also shared a bond when he told me that his greatest joy in life had been hiking in the Alps as a young man.

For a number of years, I have done a class at the Longy School of Music combining chamber music and art song, trying to encourage a cross-pollination of different mediums - a bit like living on that New Hampshire farm with art, poetry and music comingled and Mr. McDonald and Mr. Heinz enjoying each others' company. In that song and chamber music class, there were several experiments which yielded surprising results. I include them here with the hope that we as teachers continue to try things that might grant unexpected riches or nothing at all beyond the attempt. Ordinarily in the class we might read the poem set by the composer in the original language and then in English translation.

Here are four of the experiences we had together:

- The first involved "Der Atlas" from Schubert's *Schwanengesang* where Atlas is howling about carrying the entire weight of the world upon his shoulders. Both readings of the poem were more utilitarian than dramatic, at which point I asked if someone would be willing to declaim the Heine poem while the pianist played the keyboard part full of thunderous tremolos and the like. A cellist stood up and bellowed the text in a manner worthy of any raging storm in King Lear. The effect on how the singer and pianist then presented the song was staggering.
- It so happened that the same cellist was in the class a year later when we were working on Schumann's *Liederkreis*, Op. 39 set to Eichendorff poetry. The particular song we were looking at was number eight, "In der Fremde", a seemingly naive setting of a girl wandering lost in a garden, a distant castle, a love who should be there, but has been dead for so long - the final line repeated three times (Schumann's choice). As I thought about the girl's disorientation in the poem, I had a visual flashback to Ophelia having lost her wits and wandering in the fog at the end of Laurence Olivier's movie version of Hamlet. I mentioned this to our class and asked the cellist, whose hair was neatly up in a bun, whether she would consider

disheveling her hair and then read the poem for us. Again, a rare experience, but dangerously close to that fragile boundary where creativity can verge on manipulation. For instance, I would be loath to test someone's memory by either turning off the lights or taking away their music.

- One day, a wonderful soprano and pianist brought to our class "The Kingfisher" from Ravel's *Histoires Naturelles.* This singer had started our semester off by exclaiming that the Debussy String Quartet, which was also part of our project, had been one of her favorite pieces since childhood - a great way to set the atmosphere for cross-over enthusiasm. The Renard story which Ravel set is about the most beautiful blue kingfisher landing on a fisherman's rod, perhaps thinking it was the branch of a tree. Ravel's tempo marking is "*on ne peut plus lent*" (one could not go any slower) and the atmosphere is one of suspended magical disbelief. On the spur of the moment, I asked the singer and pianist to try and read the French and the English simultaneously not knowing what might transpire. What did happen, without trying to coordinate, was an extraordinary shared pacing, sense of wonder, the air in their lungs almost like two violinists or a string quartet with a single bow.
- Once we were working on the Schubert song "Vor meiner Wiege" and someone in the class who was not familiar

with the song read a translation of the poem enchantingly. However, there was a wonderful shift in tone when I asked her to read the poem in minor. This reminded me of a similar experience, years ago, when someone read a translation of a lavish Strauss love song in a fairly perfunctory way, and when I asked them to read the poem in G-Flat major the change was astonishing.

CHAPTER TEN

Teaching as Conversation

IF PART OF CREATIVE teaching for me is to help students identify and protect their ideals, to help them find the courage to make choices in the language of music, conversation that invites but does not demand is at the crux of it all. I would say that to demand conversation is inherently contradictory. Even when dealing with - or especially when dealing with the shyest individual - conversation can only be encouraged or welcomed. I remember asking a class for reactions to a passage in the Beethoven C Minor Violin Sonata, where the violinist was playing somewhat militantly and the pianist not at all so. Imagine my joy when a girl in my class said, "Well, it's the kind of passage you might be tempted to play with pride, but I'd prefer it to be more playful."

From the first movement, Beethoven C Minor Violin Sonata, Op. 30 no. 2

What a gem! After that, the two players started to notice each other a bit more, to come up with a shared choice.

Hopefully my tone and attitude working on a trio with a student ensemble would be similar to a situation where I was the pianist with two colleagues. This leads naturally to the first of many recurrent ideas that I would like to focus on. Let's start with the idea of any two, three or four people going out for lunch. Isn't it obvious that the conversation, the tone, the silences, the initiatives depend on who is sitting at the table? I would urge all of us, teachers especially, every time we offer a suggestion or criticism (a word full of negative potential) to take into account to whom we are talking. Some people say what needs to be said. Isn't it possible to be forthright and yet realize that you never need to address two different people the same way? If you want to be heard, this awareness may serve your selfish interest. A related thought that occurs to me frequently is that whoever is offering the idea being considered in a rehearsal should not be of importance - the idea itself is, and this can help avoid the kind of scorekeeping which ends up with, "We did what you wanted at letter B, how about doing what I want here." In fact, I would also encourage people to be leery of compromise if it means doing something without conviction. Being flexible and malleable is one thing, but compromise is another word with tricky connotations.

CHAPTER TEN

Leading & Cueing

One of the most frequently asked questions we hear from students is, "Who should lead?" The answers to this (notice the plural) are endless and include all aspects of cueing, which element in the music conducts the passage, voicing, relationships between rhythm and melody, players' familiarity with each other and the piece, any given player's given inclination or disinclination to lead, etc. Natural answers to the initial question might include lead together, whoever has the primary role, or whoever is in the mood to do so. Imagine the excitement of three musicians starting Beethoven's "Ghost" Trio if there is not a predetermined leader.

Beethoven Piano Trio "Ghost" in D Major, Op. 70 no.1

In that case, whoever is the instigator needs to gauge the response of the others. Robert Koff, one of the founding members of the Juilliard Quartet, supposedly said that all leading is following and vice versa. I would almost take that one step beyond and say that following, because it tends to be passive, is often counterproductive. Those who follow tend to be late, less communicative and to produce less sound.

I cannot tell you the number of times two people in a duo sonata class I teach start the opening of the Beethoven D Major or A Minor or C Minor violin sonatas and the pianist looks over for permission from the violinist to begin. It makes me want to drape a white napkin over the pianist's forearm to turn him into a butler. I remember once working on the Beethoven A Major Cello Sonata, whispering into a cellist's ear to sit on the fermata "E" at the end of the short ad libitum cello cadenza early in the first movement, until the pianist was willing to interrupt, to relish that rudeness. I believe it turned out to be the longest fermata ever heard in that spot.

Ad libitum, first movement, Beethoven A Major Cello Sonata, Op. 69

The issue of leading and taking the initative is clearly linked to the process of cueing and the apportioning of rhythm and melody. The word itself "cue" seems to imply something specific or rhythmic which is why it may not be an appropriate term for preparing a melodic gesture. Consider those last two words - the softness of diction, how long it takes to say them. Non-singers don't talk about diction much, yet the relationship between speech and singing permeates all music. Notice, on the other hand, how we speak the words clarity, articulation, motif - most likely drier and more specific. In general, rhythm is drier than melody, its components more detailed and its preparation skinnier and more defined. The trouble with skinnier cues is that there is less response time for all the players to participate. Here are three fast movement examples from the Scherzos of Schubert's "Trout" Quintet, Cello Quintet and Schumann's Piano Quartet, where a double-hitched cue might help resolve this problem.

Scherzo, Schubert "Trout" Quintet, D. 667

Scherzo, Schubert Cello Quintet, D. 956

Scherzo, Schumann Piano Quartet, Op. 47

One person can show a discreet conductorial extra beat (using eyebrow, elbow, anything that works) with the actual cue, which springs the group into action, totally shared. This shared cue, and all cues really, hopefully reveals the nature and dynamic of what is upcoming.

Obviously, the choices between melodic and rhythmic motivation are not always black and white - they can coexist and they can be ambiguous. Certainly, a non-melodic rhythmic figure like the cello opening of the Scherzo in Beethoven's Op. 59 no.1 string quartet could as easily be someone knocking on your front door:

Allegretto vivace e sempre scherzando.

Scherzo, Beethoven String Quartet, Op. 59 no.1

On the other hand, notes which are pleading or harmonies which express yearning are unlikely to be played staccato regardless of an indicated dot. It is amazing how often pianists stop, or are told to stop pedaling every time they see a dot. How reassuring it is that a dot or *sforzando* could just as well lead us to something caressed or infused with extra *vibrato*, as something brusque or virtually a punch in the gut. "It depends" - often with harmony being a primary indicator. The intrigue lies in figuring out what you want in any case.

When teaching, I love to say, "Don't decide what you like while I'm in the room", or "I know what I like but I'm not playing". More and more those two words "it depends" seem more creative than wishy-washy because what is implied is response to context and the idea that ultimately notation in music means what we perceive it to mean, as long as we are not self-serving. For instance, what does the dot signify at the end of the first figure in the Beethoven C Minor Violin Sonata?

Beethoven C Minor Violin Sonata, Op. 30 no. 2

Let's say you hear it as a Schubertian melodic gesture - then the last note is unlikely to truncate the sigh by being too short. The preparation in this case might be a measure wide and the silence afterward fluid. But if the figure is a dramatic rhythmic motif the dot might almost become an accent, the cue - perhaps one quarter note in length - precise and the silence afterwards frozen. I believe most musicians would choose the latter - an intense *piano* dynamic wishing it could be *forte* - but I think we should be careful not to disdain the former, if chosen.

If there is a shared curiosity involved in all these choices, try talking to string players about using more pedal, or pianists about searching for the perfect bow stroke. It can work. Consider how similar shifting from position to position on the cello is to leaping on the piano - free flight and the memory of space as it relates to sound.

CHAPTER TWELVE

Eye Contact

One aspect of chamber music which I think is vastly overrated is eye contact. Let's start here by returning to a sports analogy. When a pitcher in baseball struggles with his control or a basketball player loses fluidity at the free throw line, you often hear an announcer say that they are "aiming the ball". Isn't this very similar to a cellist watching a shift, stiffness taking over as the landing is aimed instead of trusted? One of the problems with orchestras is that most conductors want to be looked at all the time, both by the players and the audience. I remember conducting a Schubert symphony years ago and urging the violas to stop looking at me because looking for instructions was making them aim.

I think this happens a lot in chamber music. Often, players look at each other at the moment where trust is lacking. How nice it would be if someone looked at you with the feeling,

"Here comes this wonderful passage we get to play together" rather than, "This better be together or else." How often has one of us had the experience in a performance when someone looks at you and your reaction is, "Uh-oh, what did I do wrong?" On the other hand, there are times when you almost refuse to look at your partner so that your internal radar does not get threatened. A perfect example of this is at the end of the slow movement of the last Beethoven cello sonata where, after an elaborate florid section, time virtually comes to a standstill as the two players travel forward together in distended slow motion. In this instance, I would prefer to play with closed eyes and risk not being together than getting everything to line up by looking.

End of the slow movement, Beethoven Cello Sonata, Op. 102 no. 2

Speaking of looking, watch a piano trio sometime and notice how often the violinist sits parallel to the keyboard with the cellist on the periphery and notice how much more frequently the pianist gives eye contact to the violinist. How often do I plead, "Don't forget the cellist!" Because violinists tend to lead, and think they should, they produce more sound. Why not lead from the bottom, especially if a passage is dark or wants structural support? In most of the major piano trios, be it Mendelssohn, Schubert or Brahms, there are extended passages where the violin and cello have melodies together, separated by one or two octaves, with the piano in a supporting role. A nice way to get away from the cello being a shadow voice is to have the cellist and pianist play through these passages as cello sonatas, then after retraining the ear, add the violin. The shift in the mixture of sound can be very satisfying.

CHAPTER THIRTEEN

𝄐

Watching Concerts

CERTAINLY CONNECTED TO THE idea of looking, and not looking, is that we go to concerts to watch as well as listen. Maybe we close our eyes, but if there is excitement or interruption, we tend to watch. Comic gesture or mimed gesture or inebriated gesture needs to be seen. If Kandinsky said that his paintings were to be listened to, take the middle movements of the Debussy violin or cello sonatas and in their fantastical imaginative world watch a little - and because they are non-programmatic there is no need to define what is being conjured up. This undefined aspect of the visual and evocative can be as much fun to portray as a singer describing Pulcinella, Scaramouche and the half-naked girl in search of her handsome Spanish pirate in Debussy's setting of Verlaine's *Fantoches*.

FANTOCHES

Scaramouche et Pulcinello
Qu'un mauvais dessein rassembla,
Gesticulent noirs sous la lune
Cependant l'excellent docteur Bolonais
Cueille, avec lenteur des simples
Parmi l'herbe brune
Lors sa fille, piquant minois
Sous la charmille, en tapinois
Se glisse demi-nue
En quête de son beau pirate espagnol,
Dont un amoureux rossignol
Clame la détresse à tue-tête

PHANTOMS

Scaramouche and Pulcinella,
Whom wicked intentions have brought together,
Are dark figures, gesticulating in the moonlight,
While the excellent Doctor from Bologna
Is leisurely gathering healing herbs in the dark grass,
While his pertly pretty daughter,
Beneath the bowers, stealthily
Glides, scantily dressed,
In quest of her handsome Spanish pirate,
Whose distress an amorous nightingale
Proclaims at the top of its voice.

I do remember, once, mentioning this song to a group working on the similarly sassy, Spanish-flavored second movement of the Debussy Quartet and believe the cellist became the designated pirate - the second violinist his prize (none of this my doing, I must say).

In the eleventh Bartók Bagatelle for solo piano, he notates delayed landings on bars 2,4,9,11,13 - why? Maybe the peasant on his way home, after a lot to drink, stumbles or hiccups - definitely not an eyes-closed experience.

Bartok Bagatelle, Op. 6 no. 11

If music is restless or agitated, I think both players and listeners sit in their chairs differently than if the music is serene. In teaching, the tricky part here is that no two musicians have the same body language as they play and yet there is a natural choreography, which can even be theatrical, which enables us to communicate. Most quartets don't figure out this choreography the way a dance company does, but I believe it is inherent in a cohesive approach. Imagine the spaces between the fragments in the Agitato movement of Schumann's A Major Opus 41 no. 3 String Quartet. The instability and motion during the silences demand a physical language which is surely visual.

Agitato movement, Schumann String Quartet in A Major, Op.41 no. 3

If any of the four players looked passive they would seem as out of place as the blackmailer in Hitchcock's tennis scene in *Strangers on a Train*, whose eyes are fixed on his victim as the crowd follows the ball back and forth.

I had a very disconcerting experience at Harvard years ago coaching a marvelous violinist playing first in Beethoven's

Opus 59 no. 2 quartet. His demeanor, and seemingly his metabolism, during the heartbeat of the slow movement and during the exuberance of the Finale appeared identical, and as much as I exhorted him to visually reveal the difference, it was a struggle for him and somewhat frustrating for myself as well.

When Sviatoslav Richter is asked, in the extraordinary film *Richter the Enigma*, how he felt about being watched on stage, he essentially said he would just as well play in a pitch black space. Some strands of music, like Sarabandes in Bach cello suites, may be magical under the cover of night, but usually there is much to see and the fact that orchestra auditions are behind curtains these days heightens the impersonality and inhumanity of the process. I wish music schools, in their outreach programs, would send students out to perform at schools for the deaf.

CHAPTER FOURTEEN

Imitation, Mimicry & Awareness

THERE IS A LONG history of master-apprentice relationships in the arts and imitation can be a valuable tool in the learning process. Even with a composer as radically individualistic as Beethoven, one finds that his earliest compositions borrow from the style of predecessors such as Haydn and Mozart. Although I have little interest in students accepting everything I have to say (and get noticeably nervous if I see them write down a suggestion before assessing whether they like it or not) I have become recently intrigued by the relationship between creativity and mimicry. To truly match what another musician has just done, or is doing with you at the moment, takes phenomenal awareness, and this awareness, which can be instantaneous even in sight-reading, is at the essence of creativity.

It reminds me of taking a tennis lesson years ago with Tim Gallwey, who wrote *The Inner Game of Tennis*. There was no talk of positioning or stroke, but rather awareness of what the ball looked like, its color and lettering, and maybe a visualization of the backhand of a favorite player from the past. Now, if I see a student not breathe before a phrase, or suddenly truncate its ending, what better way to imagine the concept of preparation, impulse and follow-through than to picture Roger Federer's forehand in tennis? Here we are - sports and music again.

Let me pick a few examples where mimicry and/or awareness are essential and not as easy as one might expect:

- Opening of Mozart's Violin Sonata in B-flat, K. 454 - some of the issues here are: do both players roll the chords; if the gesture is declamatory how to match the diction and decay of each speaking point; is the dotted rhythm over-dotted; and why does Mozart differentiate the lengths of the last chord - a lot of things to consider for something that is not basically complex. Speaking of the last chord, musicians often look at each other to determine when a chord terminates, but if something expires, it may be indeterminate as sound meets silence - therefore no cutoff is warranted.

Opening, Mozart Violin Sonata, K. 454

- Tiny bridge figures in the two Dvorák piano quartets pass like a baton from player to player - the mimicry here being to match the clarity of the first example and the sigh-like quality of the second.

From the first movement, Dvorák E-flat Major Piano Quartet, Op. 87

From the Finale, Dvorák D Major Piano Quartet, Op. 23

- Two places in the Beethoven Cello Sonata, Op. 102 no.1 - the beginning of each Allegro:

From the Allegro vivace, Beethoven Cello Sonata, Op. 102 no. 1

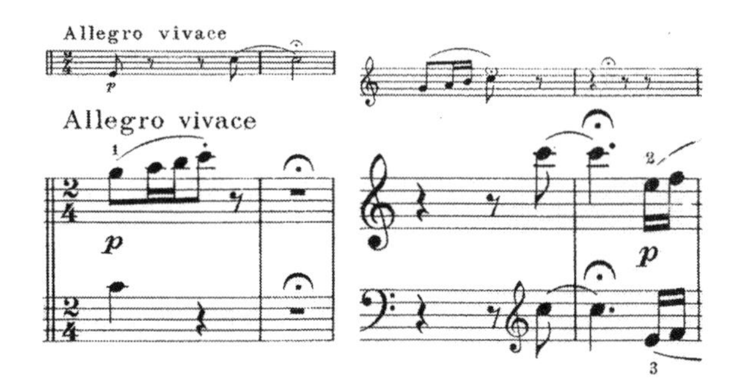

Allegro vivace, Beethoven Cello Sonata, Op. 102 no. 1

In the first case, the challenge is to match the spacing, diction and intensity of the ascending line and then matching the rhythmic integrity of the descending pattern. Again, it seems simple but it is harder than it seems, especially when the pedal can disguise what the pianist's hands are doing. In the beginning of the last movement, there is a tiny scale fragment followed by a chime tone, then the passage is repeated with the piano and cello roles reversed. Try simply isolating the chime tone so that the bow and the struck key can find the same quality of impulse - it is fun.

- Where direct imitation or canon occurs, matching approach is especially vital. In the first movement of Brahms' G Minor Piano Quartet, I would say that in order to reveal the imitation the four-note figure should highlight the upper note regardless of what beat it is on.

From the first movement, Brahms G Minor Piano Quartet, Op. 25

- In one of the most perfect canons ever conceived - the third movement of Bach's A Major Sonata for Violin and

Harpsichord - I would encourage the second person in not to ornament too differently, if one wants to recognize the canon. It is, in any case, a challenge since the underlying harmonies have wandered so far astray by the time the second voice enters.

Third movement, Bach A Major Sonata for violin and harpsichord, BWV 1015

- One exception for me might be in the finale of Schumann's Piano Quartet where, if the piano matches the bow articulations, this canonic passage can sound quite naked and raw - by adding a bit more pedal the resonance of the whole passage can truly benefit.

From the Finale, Schumann Piano Quartet, Op. 47

- Compare the opening of Beethoven's String Quartet Opus 59 no.1 with the opening Allegro in Mozart's "Dissonance" Quartet.

Opening, Beethoven String Quartet, Op. 59 no.1

From the Allegro, Mozart C Major String Quartet, K. 465

The Beethoven is marked *dolce* (for the cello anyway) and the Mozart is not, but perhaps the Mozart is actually the more dolce of the two. What does this do to the eighth note articulations in the accompanying voices? Here again we have a case where a sweeter approach would ask for a brush stroke whereas a more rhythmic approach would be drier. I remember coaching a quartet of doctors who could not get the opening of the Beethoven together until the second violinist cued the beginning instead of the cellist, at which point the group found a rhythmic cohesion. And doesn't this return us to "who should lead" and "it depends"?

- Once in a while, even playing *dolce* can become generic and I would like to think that the affect of a passage leads us to the choice of stroke, not the other way around. I have been told I like the word wistful, and think I probably do. Years ago at Boston University's Tanglewood Institute, when I asked about the transition from the moody opening of the "Dissonance" Quartet into the Allegro one of the violinists said: "I feel hopeful."

Transition from the Adagio introduction to the Allegro, Mozart C Major String Quartet, K. 465

In a teaching studio I share on the third floor of the Longy School of Music, a poster with a Daniel Barenboim quote has hung on the wall for years - "*The worst crime against music is to play mechanically.*" I understand what he is after, but my reaction - "It depends". Here are a few examples where composers seemingly use mechanical devices as an expressive foil to what is heart-rending or exalted, or even what keeps time, relative to what is timeless.

From the Andante, Mozart Violin Sonata in E-flat Major, K. 380

From the third movement, Fauré Piano Quartet in G Minor, Op. 45

Allegretto vivace e sempre scherzando.

Second movement, Beethoven String Quartet, Op. 59 no. 1

Third movement, Beethoven String Quartet, Op. 59 no.1

Opening of Variation I from the last movement,
Beethoven Piano Sonata, Op. 109

Opening of Variation II from the last movement,
Beethoven Piano Sonata, Op. 109

Again, we have the objective - subjective quandry. In the above examples, how do we determine what is, or is not a "mechanical" device?

CHAPTER FIFTEEN

What is Memory?

What is memory? If you asked a roomful of musicians this question, the conversation would hopefully be quite stimulating. It is a different question from how we memorize a given piece of music. In that case, it might involve form (A-B-A, Rondo, etc.) harmony, sense memory (e.g., fingerings), photographic memory (where something lies on the page) or "whatever helps" (a favorite response of mine). But memory might also be what enables us to phrase, to remember physical shapes, what it is that makes the space/sound relationship in that cello shift we talked about before akin to a leap on the piano. It may be a chickadee remembering the path from a tree branch to a bird feeder or hawks remembering migratory patterns. As a pianist, there are chords - say a C major triad in its three positions - that I have probably played thousands of times and now, even while out walking in the woods, I retain an indelible memory of those chords and their sensation in my hand. That recall of malleable shape feels similar to potters working clay, making vases or bowls for years on end. While the shapes and how to form them are part of memory, the aesthetics tend to be variable and this is why one of my closest friends, who is a potter, thinks of his work as being close to jazz. Again the perpetual question arises for us as artists: What is it we improvise, what is it we are willing to "not know"?

Memory is perhaps my saying to you, "Every morning I take a cold shower before putting on the kettle for tea." Not a fabulous sentence unto itself, but interesting in that I probably had those fourteen words memorized before I uttered the word "every". When we are in our mother tongue, or a familiar language, this is likely to be true. Even in sight-reading music, a distinction can be drawn between fluency (the usual description) and memory. Begin with the thought that you cannot play a phrase unless you read a phrase. That for me implies, at the very least, immediate short-term memory. If the information in a phrase is modest enough, our ability to express it has an immediate capacity for memory and this allows us to breathe, to distribute the bow, etc. In teaching, I notice how often people sight-read in a syllable-by-syllable, word-by-word manner and accept this language constriction because "they don't know it yet". I would encourage four people, reading a Haydn quartet for the first time, to bask in the pleasure of the first-time-can-only-truly-happen-once and, in a way, play "by memory" as they sight-read. It is what we do in any conversation. Obviously this access to the immediacy of language will be harder for most people playing Schönberg than Mozart or for most pianists because of the amount of information we must ingest. Ultimately, our memory tells us, reading Mozart, "I've seen or heard this before" (much like looking out a window and recognizing the patterns on a maple tree). And we don't need to translate any more. Perhaps get someone to practice their instrument with a newspaper or a book of stories by their stand and see if any parallels exist. Is phrasing in music at all like reading:"In the bottom of the ninth inning last night at Fenway Park, the bases were loaded and David Ortiz homered to win the game"? I'll bet anybody slightly familiar with baseball or English could memorize those 24 words at sight.

There is a fascinating aspect of memory that relates to how chamber music asks us to take responsibility for the whole conception of any given work. It is a violinist, playing a Beethoven sonata, knowing everything in the piano part and making choices based on that, including the so-called physical choices like fingerings. The wonderful thing about memory is the discoveries we make as we undertake the process - not that it makes us look better on stage. For me, memorizing all the little details in the orchestration of any Mozart concerto (e.g., which wind player has what at any given moment) has felt modest, whereas reaching a comparable memory state when playing the Bartók Third Concerto was a different story. All I could do there was learn something new, day by day, without getting overwhelmed by my insufficiency. It makes me wonder how many Shakespearean actors have all of Hamlet or Lear memorized - how many Hamlets have all of Ophelia's or Polonius' lines in their memory bank?

Memory itself takes an extraordinary amount of trust - what we are capable of remembering or forgetting is equally mind-boggling. If trust is at the essence of playing music with friends and colleagues, and memory includes trust and discovery, then what a shame that chamber music is so seldom played by memory! One of my richest collaborative experiences was, back in the early Nineties, playing all the Beethoven and Brahms cello sonatas by memory with a close friend, Paul Cohen, in a number of recitals. The sense of trust, interdependence, discovery and yes, vulnerability, was certainly heightened every time we played. Heightened experience is at the heart of performing. Rarely do we reach the same degree of inspiration in the privacy of our living room as we do on stage. It may be the reason we accept the fear that can be part of the bargain.

In my time at Harvard, I did have two groups that decided, without my urging, to memorize what they were working on

(Barber's *Summer Music* for Woodwind Quintet and Debussy's String Quartet). In both cases, the performances were exhilarating and liberating. These were people playing music out of sheer joy, not obligation, and probably not a single music major amongst them. I have thought often since then how obligation can drain us of joy and how little choice students have in what they play, what they study, and with whom they play. When those Harvard students picked their colleagues and repertoire, the question asked so often in conservatories, "Do we have to perform?" became, "When do we get to perform?" I felt blessed and did not even have to give grades.

In those years at Harvard, I probably coached at least 300 chamber groups, virtually all of which performed entire works at the end of semesters, whether it be a Bartok Quartet, Schubert or Enescu Octets or a Mozart Wind Serenade. One such group, consisting of a religion major, an economics major, a political science major and a chemistry major, learned, in one semester, the Brahms C Minor, Prokofiev Second and Beethoven Op. 18, no. 6 String Quartets. In that particular ensemble the two violinists went on to have distinguished careers in music, but, for the most part, most of the people I worked with pursued other paths, perhaps to protect their love for music.

Before moving on from this conversation about memory, it occurs to me that many of our recollections of concerts we have gone to years ago tend to be as visual as aural, which reinforces the idea that we do watch concerts. For me, it could be the indelible image of Mischa Schneider of the Budapest Quartet, hunched over his cello, playing the *pizzicatos* in the slow movement of Beethoven's Op. 59 no. 3 Quartet, or of Rudolf Serkin levitating from his piano bench as he started the last movement of Beethoven's "Emperor" Concerto. It could be my memory of sitting high up in Carnegie Hall listening to Myra Hess play the last three Beethoven piano sonatas. Often we say, when hearing music in small intimate spaces, "This is how it was meant to be" but, even though I have a faint memory of how luminous her sound was 55 years ago, what I truly retain is the picture of this mythic figure miles away - the separation making the experience more magical, not less.

One more thought regarding memory - notice how differently we talk when recounting something from the distant past, than when we are in the present tense. If there is a sense of nostalgia, our tone changes, we are less hurried and have more air in our voice. Compare saying, "I made eggs for breakfast this morning" with "When I was a child my mother used to make me eggs." As a string player, you might use more bow speed or play over the fingerboard, as a pianist you would probably use more pedal and perhaps the soft pedal. If there is no poem to indicate a time frame, whether or not a musical context is about memory is yet another subjective choice for us to make.

CHAPTER SIXTEEN

"Letting Go" Approaches to Earlier Music

MANY TIMES WHEN RECURRENT ideas occur to me in teaching, it is in "older" music like Bach or Mozart where there is a carryover from prevalent performing styles which today feel outdated. For me, there is a wonderful connection between the physical and emotional world in how we play earlier music, especially as it is encouraged in period instrument circles. The key distinction here is between "holding on to" and "letting go of". In life, ask most people which of these is freer and healthier and the answer is predictable. Why not in music? Sometimes the simplest words can surprise us in the depth of their connotations. In Stanley Ritchie's book on baroque violin practices, *Before the Chinrest*, he says he prefers to no longer use the term bow "hold" or "grip" for obvious reasons. Let's make an equation which has letting go equaling "up" (anti-gravity) and holding onto equaling "down" (gravity) and then think about the relationship between physical principles and our emotional condition. And, if something is up or uplifting, imagine the gait of an animal such as a horse or a deer as you play the rhythms in the outer movements of the Schubert B-flat Trio.

From the first movement, Schubert B-flat Trio, D. 898

From the last movement, Schubert B-flat Trio, D. 898

Isn't it true that the animal is up in the air on the long tones with the hooves touching the ground lightly on the short notes? There is joy and breath in release, and CPE Bach's idea that long notes last half their notated value makes so much sense when you exhale and "let go".

Several years ago, in a Beethoven duo-sonata class I was teaching, it so happened that both pianists were sick so, unexpectedly, a violinist volunteered to play the Bach *Chaconne*. We had an amazing two-hour session together. His influences had been old-school Russian with fairly predictable tendencies, but he was more than open to trying different approaches. After an hour or so, he had a look of surprise and said, "I'm not tired - I'm usually exhausted by now." I was ecstatic as I saw what "letting go" could accomplish.

What I find myself fighting against, especially in teaching Bach, is that most musicians are trained to sustain sound, that beauty and legato are considered one and the same and that vibrato is a vital component of this beauty. Equally problematic is the concept of the "big line". To begin with, the word "line" for me implies tension. One does not travel from point A to point B in music in a straight line unless one is seeking tension. Surely one wants a vision of a phrase, an extended passage, a view of large sections and entire movements, but legato is not necessarily the answer. To articulate multiple times in a phrase need not interrupt or jeopardize the phrase. It enhances and flavors through diction.

With this in mind, I will often offer the idea that the places that are most expressive and inflected in Mozart might be the places to be least legato and thereby reveal the feature of interest. A dissonance might be shown by placing it late, getting rid of vibrato and actually lifting the bow from the string (which is easier at the frog) to create the speaking point. This is a big adjustment for most students and it can be challenging to get a violinist to practice making a beautiful, supple bow change which includes this silence. Another idea that resurfaces over and over is to think bow first, then the left hand. Our breath comes from the bow and it is interesting to notice how excessive vibrato can interfere with the bow's flight through space. This is not to imply that one would ever want to separate the sensations of the bow from the left hand. In fact, I notice frequently that string players tend to be more in tune when the bow is comfortable and that group intonation also has everything to do with sympathetic bow approach. Recently, I was encouraging a wonderful young cellist to make an expressive bow change and she looked surprised, saying that she had never thought of a bow change in that way.

Part of the issue here is identifying what is ornamental in music. What I always encourage is the idea that ornaments and gestures have a natural release and therefore cannot travel too slowly or intensely. Ornaments can be trills, turns, mordents, but they can also be scales, groups of notes, or even vibrato. Ornamentation, especially in Bach, can be a way of traveling from one structural long tone to another. Look at the opening of the fifth Bach Cello Suite:

Prelude, Fifth Cello Suite, Bach BWV 1011

After the first octave, if the little notes are played as an ornament, there can be found a wonderful momentum towards the next intense chord. Played melodically, as it often is, it might take twice as long to go from bar line to bar line.

Look at the first violin part in the opening of the Mozart K. 136 Divertimento:

Opening, Mozart Divertimento, K. 136

The two little flagged figures are obvious ornaments but more importantly the sixteenth notes under a slur - four times the same thing - become an extended ornament which implies *decrescendo* and motion. Another thought that may be helpful in revealing an ornament - avoid *legato* on either side of it. Imagine a C major scale in Mozart followed by a trill - they are two different features and want to be recognized as such.

One last idea I would like to include here is that if slurs are gestures, most of the time they have implied *decrescendos* which is one reason Mozart did not use decrescendos in his notation. According to Leopold Mozart, the first note in a slur (at least in relatively short slurs) is the strongest, with each successive note being weaker. This was expected practice. It is vital to trust the length of slurs in any Mozart edition because most of the time the slurs themselves indicate natural bowings and articulations. If the slur length makes the bow feel cramped maybe the tempo is too slow. And as Stanley Ritchie used to say to me in andantes or adagios in Mozart violin sonatas, "Don't call it a slow movement."

Not long ago I observed Stanley working with a group of students at the Garth Newel Music Center in Virginia and was struck by his suggesting that: "All music is in one". At the time, it seemed a bit far-fetched, but since then I have become obsessively aware of how this is essentially a plea for gesture. The conductor who micro-manages, subdivides incessantly as a way of controlling synchronicity. Being in one helps unequalize beats in a measure creating contour. Stanley was working on Baroque repertoire at the time, but let me apply his idea to three places in Beethoven quartets where I imagine most groups would ordinarily subdivide - the introduction to Op. 59 no. 3 and the opening Allegro statements of the "Harp" and Op. 130 quartets. The latter two examples might lose a little rhythmic starch but what they would gain is most appealing to me - the "Harp" more welcoming and less militant, Op. 130 having more sweep.

Introduction, Beethoven String Quartet, Op. 59 no. 3

Opening Allegro from the "Harp" Quartet

Opening Allegro from Op. 130

Speaking of quartets, when you are done with Beethoven, consider the Beatles' song *Eleanor Rigby*. In one?

CHAPTER SEVENTEEN

Dynamics in Mozart

OFTEN, WHEN TEACHING OR rehearsing, you find yourself saying, "Let's try this one more time" and know that you are bound to try it at least five more times - again, the inefficiency of the creative process. So, one more thought I talk a lot about in Mozart concerns dynamics. Certainly the nature of instruments during Mozart's lifetime affected the dynamic range possible in his music, therefore making articulation even more significant as an expressive outlet. But beyond this, *piano* and *forte* are just as variable as the dots and *sforzandos* we looked at before. Sometimes they are about strong dynamic contrast, but just as often they indicate the contours or nuances of a phrase, or points of impulse.

An example of true contrast from the K. 481 E-flat Violin Sonata:

An example of contour-nuance from the K. 379 G Major Violin Sonata:

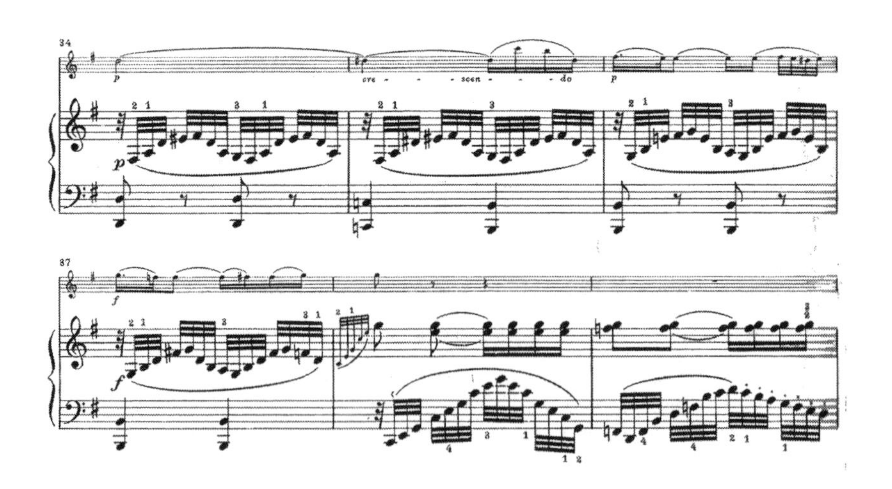

An example of rhythmic impulse from the K. 378 B-flat Violin Sonata:

Mozart's music is the perfect model for adjusting notation to context and seeking what is natural. In the Clarinet Trio K. 498, for example, I would think that the *fortes* in measures 49 and 51 apply only to the new entry in the left hand of the keyboard part. Otherwise, the other voices would end up stressing the un-weighted resolution of the previous phrase.

From the first movement, Mozart Clarinet Trio, K. 498

In Beethoven, however, there is always the chance or likelihood that notation will lead you in the direction of unnatural choices. It would be almost unimaginable for any of us to come up with Beethoven's dynamic schemes on our own. They are too idiosyncratic and asymmetrical. No two crescendos last the same number of measures and sometimes they go beyond the point of harmonic tension. Look at this passage in the G Minor Cello Sonata where the crescendo lasts one measure too long:

From the Beethoven Cello Sonata in G Minor, Op. 5 no. 2

3

CHAPTER EIGHTEEN

The Mozart - Beethoven Polarity

THERE ARE ENDLESS IDEAS which symbolize the polarities between Mozart and Beethoven. If the nature of rhythm and counterpoint is largely vertical and that of melody essentially horizontal, then Beethoven is intrinsically pianistic and vertical, Mozart violinistic and vocal. In Beethoven, it is often appropriate for a pianist to actually hit a key or for a violinist's bow to bite the string - in Mozart, virtually never. This is not to ignore wind playing. To begin with, I find idiomatic woodwind writing all over Mozart piano sonatas and violin sonatas, and it can be fun to ask two students playing a violin sonata how they would tongue a particular passage.

Take measures 5-7 in the introduction to the B-flat Violin Sonata K. 454 and compare it to the opening of the Adagio of the Serenade for 13 Winds and see what it does to the conception of sound.

From the Introduction, Mozart B-flat Violin Sonata, K. 454

Adagio, Mozart Serenade for 13 Winds, K. 361

Can a pianist sound like the woodwind underbelly with its basset horns? On the other hand, can the oboist's B-flat sneak in with an upbow?

One more idea regarding Mozart and Beethoven I like to emphasize in teaching, is that often in Mozart a *forte* might be an enhanced or warmer *piano* whereas a *piano* in Beethoven might be a repressed or compressed *forte*. How many times do we hear performances of Mozart where all the *fortes* intensify or of Beethoven, where as soon as there is a *piano* the intensity vanishes?

A wonderful exercise I try from time to time is to practice scales where crescendos relax and decrescendos intensify. It's not easy but can be helpful and revealing. The "relaxing crescendo" is perhaps a good model for the transition back to the recapitulation of the first movement of the Brahms G Major Violin Sonata where, as the music gets ostensibly louder and faster, the intensity of the entire middle section yields, allowing one to land home gently.

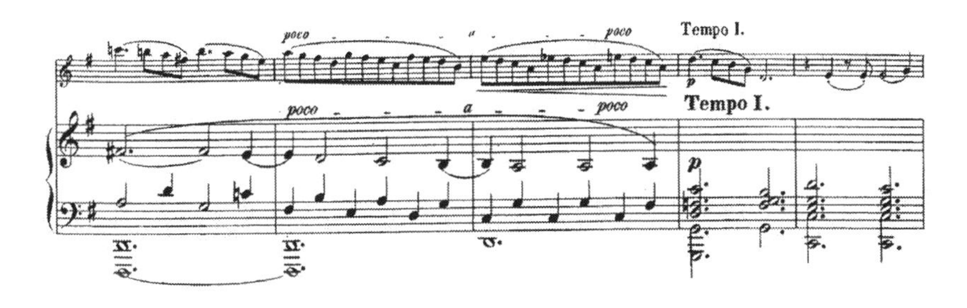

Transition to recapitulation in the first movement
Brahms G Major Violin Sonata, Op. 78

A final thought here would be: if *fortes* are not invariably intense we can retain transparency in all dynamics which can be wonderful in sunny music like Dvorák's Piano Quintet. What does it take to hear this second violin-viola playful dialogue in the first movement?

From the first movement, Dvorák Piano Quintet in A Major, Op. 81

Again, as the concepts of transparency, release and articulation resurface, it makes period instrument approaches appealing and applicable even to a Brahms or Dvorák sextet.

From the time of Bach to the present, the gap between those who compose and those who play has become wider and wider and, as a result, the sense of mutual trust has eroded. Composers in earlier times could assume that performers would have a familiarity with aspects of style, so they could under-notate. By the time the 19th century ended, virtually everything was notated, including tempos and where and how to play with freedom. This loss of trust and this over-managing of the creative process is a pity. If you think about it, one of the reasons we might connect to a particular performance of the Schubert A Minor Quartet relates to the choice of tempo. Would any two people read a given poem at the same "tempo"? Why is it that Schubert or Schumann would set the same poem of Goethe in wonderfully different ways or why is it that Schubert set Goethe's *Nur wer die Sehnsucht kennt* multiple times, all remarkably distinct? We change, music changes and its notation should not imprison us.

CHAPTER NINETEEN

Intuition - Inquiry

ONE OF THE THINGS I notice in how people approach chamber music has to do with the relationship between intuition and intellectual inquiry. I would like to think that the latter need not threaten the former and that a harmony between the two can be ideal. For any of us, our brain may connect us to a given passage whereas our heart may connect us more readily to another passage. This can be similar to the relationship between doing and listening in playing. It is critical, in teaching, to notice where analysis and definition create connection for a student or when they do the opposite. A while ago I was talking with a fellow teacher about these issues of knowledge and definition and he described watching a master class where a student was playing a Schubert sonata for someone, I believe it was Alfred Brendel, and when asked where the second subject was, could not identify it and was more or less dismissed. Is it not possible that the student who did not know the answer might nonetheless play the passage exquisitely while the one who does know the answer could end up, for all it's worth, expressively barren? My point would be that, although we probably all need some basic working vocabulary, determining what that consists of is hard to establish. I certainly have worked with people who could do a brilliant harmonic analysis of a Beethoven or Bartók quartet without it necessarily lending an expressive depth to their playing. Whereas, I have met musicians who responded to every single harmony with inflection and inspiration but God help them to describe chordal function. Sometimes it makes me want to avoid the world of definition altogether. Will actually calling something a "Neapolitan" chord help make it sadder?

Allow me, once more, to return to the Mozart - Beethoven conversation. If Mozart's compositional process has ease and Beethoven's has struggle, our manner of working invariably reflects that. I'm never sure that Mozart benefits from scrutiny while Beethoven thrives on it - here again, intuition vis-a -vis intellect. The beauty of childrens' creativity is that they can feel what we do, but have not figured out an articulated language to describe it. Some of us stay in that innocent space more than others and it is a pity if teaching imposes too much of the conscious world on the unconscious spirit.

I have a fond memory of coaching, years ago, an 11 year-old girl on a Mozart string quartet and thinking, quite awestruck, "That must be how Mozart would have sounded at that age." Then, at least 20 years later, I heard that same girl, now a woman, play a Mozart viola quintet and was profoundly disappointed by the encroachment of the adult world - the simplicity she had as a child had somehow gotten covered with a veneer. Perhaps we should be wary of progress. People in all fields expect improvement and institutions assume it - otherwise they would be out of business. Is that why DMA candidates get to play on better concert pianos, in many institutions, than undergraduate or masters students? Is that an example of misguided hierarchy?

CHAPTER TWENTY

Conscience & Art

IN A SIMILAR VEIN, imagine coaching the Shostakovich Eighth Quartet with a group of 16 year-olds or 26 year-olds or older adults. Would you assume a different departure point or approach? Not necessarily! The one common factor might be to convey an awareness of what life in the Soviet Union was like in that era, how fear and brutality could not be separated from art.

Realizing that it is inconceivable to play Shostakovich without being conscious of the climate in which he wrote, makes me wonder about our role as teachers regarding students' awareness of history, oppression and the times in which we live. In 1970, we did have demonstrations at Juilliard when the United States, under Nixon, was bombing Cambodia, even though some distinguished faculty suggested we go back to our practice rooms. I am glad we protested and now get uneasy when I hear colleagues say, "All I want to do is teach", if it means injustice is being ignored. During the cultural revolution in China, playing a Beethoven sonata could land you in a forced labor camp or jail. Should I, 40 years later, as I work on Beethoven sonatas with my eager students from China, now safely in Boston, mention the stark contrast between the two experiences? It is not an easy question and the answer seems as variable as our inclination to approach every student differently.

Certainly when discussing the integrity and significance of Bela Bartók and Pablo Casals with students I can never overlook their stands against fascism and censorship. In 1993 I played and taught in Damascus, Syria and remember playing the Fauré G Minor Quartet at a beautiful old palace (a work I have recently worked on with four Chinese students in Boston). Twelve years later I received an email from a former student from Syria, who had done her doctorate in Boston, but was back home experiencing the terror as Assad was bombing his own people and snipers were taking over her city. Her message was: "Everyone is saying Sonata Opus Seven but no one is playing it". It took me a while to realize that this was code for S.O.S., a plea for help going unheeded. Now she is in Texas, viewed by many as a potential terrorist because of her nationality. Trying to help her, mentioning her country's plight to my students perhaps is a small way of not "just wanting to teach" and a recognition that we here are not always the bastion of morality we pretend to be as we confront evil abroad.

Over the years, I have composed music without thinking of myself as a composer. I have climbed mountains without thinking of myself as a mountaineer. I have conducted without thinking of myself as a conductor. And now, although I have always thought of myself as a musician, I've been writing down these thoughts day by day without thinking of myself as a writer.

In 1984, I kept a daily journal for 4 weeks as I climbed Mt. McKinley (Denali) with two bass-player friends - we whimsically called ourselves the Juilliard Mountaineering Club. Our little home-made flag, which we would plant on summits around the world, read: *JMC Allegro ma non troppo*. Re-reading that journal more than 25 years later, I was astonished to find that the limits we tested during that odyssey included much that had apprehension, conflict, fear and exhaustion - all in relationship to beauty, serenity, interdependence and the satisfaction of attaining our goal.

Testing one's limits to the extent of going beyond safety is one thing - testing the boundaries of music interpretatively can be something curiously similar, and even perilous. What constitutes the boundaries of style from Baroque to Modern has so little consensus, and the fact that outlooks change so much from generation to generation makes it difficult to find a departure point for the teacher-student conversation regarding proper choices. What is appropriate freedom, bending of tempo, altering of articulations in Bach, Mozart, Brahms, Rachmaninoff? There are times I might ask a student, “What is the latest you can place such-and-such a bar line without sacrificing the music’s integrity?” Or ask a pianist to explore how much freedom is possible in this melodic improvisatory passage from the Dumka of Dvorák’s Piano Quintet while playing within the strings’ seemingly regular patterns:

Dumka excerpt, Dvorák Piano Quintet in A Major, Op. 81

CHAPTER TWENTY-ONE

Safety & Courage

NOTICING AND TESTING ONE'S limits on a ridge, where a fall could be the end of you, may not be so different from how a quartet might attack Beethoven's "Grosse Fuge", or a pianist's recognition that to start Beethoven's "Hammerklavier" Sonata with two hands would deny the courage which making that first leap with one hand implies. And yet the expression, "people don't take risks anymore" (because of the fear of imperfection) has become a bit worn. Perhaps courage is not just about risk but also fragility and vulnerability, letting certain accents in Schubert communicate "I cannot" instead of "I can". Maybe it can transfer some of the coolness of projection on stage to something more private.

Understanding that while there are always moments, gestures, sections in music of extreme daring, most of the chamber music/sociology bond revolves around an awareness that is softer and radiates safety. To begin with, it takes a lot of courage to walk out on stage with the belief that those listening to you wish you the best and might even forgive a mistake. When I teach, I am grateful when I see a student miss a leap or play a sour note and then smile with a sweetness that says, “I’ll get it next time”. If we realize that confidence is fragile, then destructive behavior in teaching or rehearsing is criminal. When music asks for it, we may engage in combat, but if we want to help others find the courage to make creative choices, modest or bold, without fear of judgment, the working atmosphere thrives on safety and protection. If there is a choice between being kind or being stimulating, let’s consider starting with the former and trust that the latter will take care of itself.

Here is a simple rule in chamber music, from one who hates rules: Lead from what is easiest or has the least to do. It could be a pianist helping start the third of Schumann’s *Four Fairy Tales* so the violist worries a bit less about controlling the “springing” bow.

Third of Schumann’s Four Fairy Tales for Viola & Piano, Op. 113

It could be a pianist's left hand, playing an occasional chord in Mozart, shepherding the right hand through its dozens of notes, or similarly the drawing of the bow being the primary sensation for a string player when the left hand has to navigate tricky passages. It could be a critical moment of ensemble togetherness, where the person coming in from silence "conducts" the location more easily because they are not busy playing. Usually in passagework, one might assume that if there is something ongoing it is the responsibility of the one who joins to catch what is already in motion. My experience has been that, if you shift the responsibility so that Person A includes Person B, does not take them for granted, maybe even altering timing and articulation slightly to synchronize the hitch-point, the likelihood of the passage being together is a lot higher. A good example of this might be measures 25 - 26 in the first movement of Beethoven's D Major Violin Sonata Op. 12, no. 1:

From the first movement, Beethoven D Major Violin Sonata, Op. 12 no.1

To call this another rule is a bit silly - it is just another facet of making a colleague feel wanted.

There are endless other examples of what can create a sense of safety. Certainly the fingerings we choose can have an accessibility which can be reassuring. Sometimes a pianist might add a touch of pedal to a passage because it protects an exposed leap or because it might make the violin, up on the E string, sound warmer, less raw - give it a bed to lie in, so to speak. One of the worst feelings one can have playing a passage is the sensation of trying to "catch up" to the music or to be perpetually running out of air or bow. In all these cases, imagine one's gratitude if your partner or partners recognize your need and provide either extra space or extra motion, whichever helps.

Here are two other scenarios: Imagine a performance of, let's say, a quartet, and one person has a small lapse of concentration - often there is a boomerang effect where the other players all have a lapse as well before focus is re-established, if it can be. How nice it is, after you make a mistake, if your partner does something extra loving or beautiful, not to show you up but to be reassuring. Once, playing the Poulenc Clarinet Sonata with a wonderfully creative friend, Charlie Neidich, I made a little, not terribly noticeable mistake and when he imitated the figure two measures later, put in the identical slip - his way of not showing me up but enjoying the humor of the music as a prankster should. It makes you appreciate how jazz musicians don't seem to worry about "mistakes".

There is a place in Errol Garner's live "Concert by the Sea" recording where he takes a leap and smacks a ninth on landing. Maybe he planned on an octave, didn't get it, and then put in a bunch more ninths so he could get a twinkle in his eye saying, "Gotcha". How often do we experience *that* in a classical concert?

Helping one another, protecting each other, having an awareness of others' needs, all these are as much a social process as an artistic one. When letting go of ego allows teacher and student to converse and explore together, the potential for surprise is astonishing. It is not so difficult to be kind to people. I have seen what it can do as often on a soccer field as in a chamber ensemble. Our English translation for the French word "ensemble" is "together". When teaching and learning coexist and mutuality between teacher and student becomes possible, when we are grateful to teach, then the thanks travel both ways when students eventually leave us.

CHAPTER TWENTY-TWO

Final Thoughts
(with the Help of Schubert)

PART OF THE PLEASURE of an engrossing novel or movie is the wish for it not to end. Perhaps this has been for me a kind of recollection, not of accumulated wisdom, but rather a way to avoid forgetting anything to be cherished. Many a time, I turned down a rehearsal to protect a soccer night or changed out of soccer cleats into concert garb on the way to a performance. It always seemed clear that passion for music and sports intertwined, the love for one feeding off the love for the other. The world around us can be so aggressive that to hear a Chilean soccer player say in an interview that, "It is important to treat the ball tenderly" is unexpectedly delightful. In 1971, I had the joy of watching the Brazilian magician Pelé play with his soccer club Santos in La Paz, Bolivia. His grace and understanding of his teammates was comparable to any chamber music experience I've enjoyed.

Great athletes see what is around them with astonishing awareness and recognize the needs and capabilities of their teammates. Watching Wayne Gretzky play hockey, it was clear he could see openings non-existent to the normal eye. Watching Pelé pass a soccer ball, every time it seemed to be within the natural fluid rhythm of the player running to receive the pass. Julius Erving ("Dr. J"), basketball's creative genius, supposedly said that everything he did came from improvisation.

I am reminded that when I returned from that climbing trip over thirty years ago in Alaska, people asked me: "Would you do it again?" Realizing that because the mountain and its conditions are always changing, as is the person climbing, "to do it again" is out of the question.

As musicians, we are often asked, "Who is your favorite composer?" It should be impossible to answer and many of us wind up saying, "What I'm working on or in love with at the moment." However, for me, the invariable answer has been Schubert, partly because of regret over a life cut short at 31 and the wonder over what might have been.

Here are a few Schubert examples which collectively may sum up some of what I have attempted to describe in these musings. Ordinarily, ask a musician to name an appropriate dynamic for a passionate passage and most likely they would assume *forte*. The beginning of the slow movement of the

Schubert E-flat Piano Trio is famous for its beautiful cello solo but the "surprise" for me comes a bit later when there is a passage marked *appassionato* in a *pianissimo* dynamic:

From the slow movement, Schubert E-flat Piano Trio, D. 929

How to make that texture tremble? I imagine the shimmer in the piano arpeggios, and how pedaling affects this, connects to how the string players choose to vibrate. Maybe Schubert was inspired by the memory of his Adagio for Piano Trio (also known as a *Notturno* and possibly intended as the original slow movement for the B-flat Piano Trio) where he also asked for an appassionato in a pianissimo dynamic:

Schubert Adagio for Piano Trio "Notturno", D. 897

Earlier, I talked about the opening of the Schubert Cello Quintet's slow movement, talked also about how memory affects us and about the possible harmony between our heart and our brain. There are two moments in this movement that symbolize much of what I have tried to communicate. Let's start with the premise that the word "structure" has a coldness to it, especially for the intuitive musician. But, let's temper that with the thought that memory, or what has happened to us in the past, is surely connected to emotional response. After the serene opening section with its choral writing in the inner voices, there is a trill whose growl is the link to the tumult of the middle F minor section. I remember asking students how they might relate the melody's intense long-tone A-flat here (M. 30) to the endlessly peaceful G-sharp at the beginning of the movement (see example on page 44) and how that affects the restlessness of the accompaniment (at least at the outset).

Link to the middle F minor section, slow movement,
Schubert Cello Quintet, D. 956

And, were it to be conducted, what would you want the conductor to acknowledge? As before, no single answer exists beyond the choice of the players themselves. After the storm - if you can call it that - subsides, the opening comes back, but right before the end of the movement that same trill that led us into F minor comes back and one has the feeling, "Oh, Schubert, you can't do this to us again." Although there is a fleeting reemergence of F minor, the music melts back into E major and the sense of peace is all the more touching for fear it would not be granted.

End of the slow movement, Schubert Cello Quintet, D. 956

This ultimate emotional moment is surely affected by the memory by what happened previously and the shape of the movement as a whole.

Back in the early Eighties, I was hired to teach piano at Marlboro College in Vermont and prior to meeting my students was taken out to lunch by the President. The one thing I recall him trying to impress upon me was the significance of grading. He mentioned a thank you letter he had received from a former student to whom he had given a "D", who had subsequently "become one of the most successful trial lawyers in L.A." and was now grateful for the tough grade and lesson learned because it taught him how the real world works. During the lunch I nodded a lot and then, in the years I taught there, gave "A" after "A" to kids, some of whom could barely play a C major scale. (It turns out that my potter friend I wrote about before coached the soccer team up there, and not being a student myself, I managed to score a fair number of illicit goals for the team when not teaching.)

Clearly, I am not very fond of the "real world" the President talked about, or of the kind of success he was lauding. Once, at a post-concert reception, a patron asked me if I felt my life had been a success. Inwardly cringing, I smiled and said, "Do you mean have I been content?" The conversation likely shifted pretty quickly.

Why all this? There is a wonderful Schubert song called "Greisengesang" set to a Rückert poem in which the white hair on the old man's head is likened to winter's frost. All in nature has died and Schubert reflects this austerely in the minor mode. But then, "There is a nightingale in my heart which sings to me: Shut out the harshness of reality and protect the fragrance of dreams." Does the song remain in minor here? Impossible! Even though we may respond to major and minor in Schubert in a very elemental way, there is no certainty even here. As Schubert wrote in his diary, shortly after his mother died (a dream he recorded), "I wandered off into a faraway land singing my songs and whenever I wished to sing of joy, it turned to sorrow and when I wished to sing of sorrow, it turned to joy."

As I am seemingly coming to the end of this process of putting my thoughts on paper, I have been rereading the *Serpent of Stars* (1933), a little gem of a book by Jean Giono, a wonderful author from Provence almost unknown in this country. Like many of his novels, this is an ode to nature, to a way of life, untainted by so-called civilization. At one point the "master of the beasts" turns to a young aspiring shepherd and says: "Don't think you know everything. You know the sheep, but to know is to be separate from. Now try to love; to love is to join. Then, you will be a shepherd." This somehow sums up simply and elegantly what I have tried to communicate.

It seems to me that our emotional journey through life and our journey of learning resembles Schubert's dream - happy, sad, better, worse, none of them need to be defined in finite terms. The circle which we are part of just keeps moving, and perhaps this resembles the freedom we attain when we can let go while playing music and experience perpetual motion. If my job as a teacher is to prepare my students for the real world, I worry that I may have been an abject failure, but if I have helped a few of them "protect the fragrance of dreams" it has been well worth it.

Appendix

In conjunction with this book, the author has set up a YouTube channel where a variety of live performances, both solo and collaborative, can be found, as well as coaching session videos: http://preview.tinyurl.com/y7w8curb

Solo

Bach Partita no. 6 in E Minor
Bartók Fourteen Bagatelles, Op. 6
Debussy Six Epigraphes Antiques
Harbison 4 More Occasional Pieces
Schubert Drei Klavierstücke, D. 946
Schubert Piano Sonata in A Major. (Op. Post), D. 959
Mozart A Minor Rondo, K.511

Collaborative

With Bayla Keyes, violin
Prokovfiev Sonata no. 1 in F Minor, Op. 80; Shostakovich Sonata, Op. 134

With Anya Shemetyeva, violin, viola
Bach Cantabile for violin & keyboard, BWV 1019a
Ensecu Impressions of Childhood for violin & piano
Shostakovich Viola Sonata, Op. 147

With Bonnie Thron, cello
Debussy Cello Sonata

With Paul Cohen, cello
Beethoven Sonatas in G Minor, Op.5 no. 2; D Major Op. 102 no. 2

With Jayne West, soprano
Dvorák, Gypsy Songs; Dvorák, Love Songs
Prokovfiev, Akhmatova Songs

From January 31,1986 Schubert Birthday Celebration at Symphony Space, New York City
Piano Trio in B Flat Major, D. 898 with Ruth Waterman, violin and Bonnie Thron, cello
Shepherd on the Rock, Offertory with Dawn Upshaw, soprano and Charles Neidich, clarinet
Selected Lieder with Dawn Upshaw

ABOUT THE AUTHOR

The author on the summit of Mt McKinley (Denali) in 1984.
Not in the picture, two fellow musicians from the Juilliard
Mountaineering Club, Jon Deak and Richard Hartshorne.

Robert Merfeld has lead a life in which love for music has meshed with love of the outdoors. Although his career has had him playing recitals at Alice Tully Hall, the Library of Congress and Ravinia with some of the world's most prominent musicians, he could as easily be found on a soccer field, be it Central Park in New York City or a dusty field in La Paz, Bolivia. He started playing chamber music at the age of 9 both on piano and viola. Over the past 60 years he has taught and performed this literature in places such as Marlboro Music Festival, Harvard and Boston Universities, The Longy School of Music of Bard College and Tanglewood. He has, as well, taught master classes (a term he does not favor) throughout the U.S., the Middle East, Latin America and Korea.

Made in the USA
Middletown, DE
06 July 2017